An Introduction to Biblical Dream Interpretation

Understanding How God Can Talk To You In Your Dreams

Heather Sutherland

Copyright © 2020 Heather Sutherland

All rights reserved.

ISBN:9781727205602
ISBN-13: 987-9781727205602

DEDICATION

To the memory of the man who guided me through the foothills of
spiritual dream interpretation and was the inspiration for this book
John Paul Jackson (1950 – 2015)

CONTENTS

	Foreword	7
1	My Dream Journey	9
2	Dreams in the Judeo-Christian scriptures	15
3	Types of Dream and their meaning	23
4	Why are colours important	39
5	People in dreams	43
6	Other Symbols	51
7	Remembering Your Dreams	59
8	Common Dreams	63
9	When is a dream not a dream?	67
10.	Dream Interpretation as an Evangelistic Tool	69
	Other Resources	77
	About the Author	79

FOREWORD

Reading this book will not make you a master dream interpreter.

What it will do is to reveal what for many readers, will be like a new country they have never visited before. Off the beaten track, not in the package holiday advertisements, it will make you the discovering, independent traveller of your own dream life and probably those of some of your friends and family.

In this book, my dear friend and fellow traveller, Heather Sutherland will be your local guide, showing you some wonderful sights (and insights) that you may never have stumbled on in your former travels.

My wife, Cynthia, and I have known Heather for the best part of 20 years. Early in that journey, she joined us, scarcely more than apprentices ourselves, to train as a teacher and interpreter of dreams. For two or three years, it was mostly just the three of us, sowing seeds in Scotland, of what would within another couple of years become astonishingly widespread and in another couple of years after that become almost mainstream.

We saw the interpretation of many people's dreams have significant impacts, first on their understanding and then on their lives. So how did we find ourselves able to do this?

Every story has more beginnings than we suppose but one beginning was in the 1980's when a visiting, wise and benevolent English Bishop asked a young American man, "Can you tell me what my dream means?" When he told him the meaning of his dream, after a few moments for it to sink in, he asked him the next shrewd question: "How did you do that?"

John Paul Jackson, already widely known in the USA for his startling ability to interpret dreams had never been asked that before. His answer, which he later recounted, was not nearly as shrewd, was, "Well, I just do it." David Pytches, his new Bishop friend said, "Who are you training to do what you do?" John Paul, rather surprised, replied, "I'm not training anybody." The next comment was: "That's a pity, because when you die, your gift will die with you."

That piercing comment led eventually to John Paul authoring and widely teaching a series of three courses (eventually to many thousands in many countries) and, swamped by the astonishing demand, training a diverse group of people to do what he now did, to be a teacher and dream interpreter and to train others to do the same.

In 2015 he did die but his gift by no means died with him, thank you John Paul and thank you David Pytches.

In the early years, Heather Sutherland joined us, teaching the courses and doing dream interpretation in various settings, especially in Scotland but soon also in England, Sweden and Germany. Heather has applied herself vigorously to study and practice, interpreting about 1500 dreams under evaluation from John Paul's umbrella of teachers and he eventually declared her to be a "Master Dream Interpreter," one of only two people he ever conferred that recognition on outside the USA. Thus, in latter years we started joining her teams!

With our mutual pal, fellow Scottish teacher and Master Dream Interpreter, Charity Bowman Webb, Heather set up "www.thedreamhouse.co" as an internet based interpretation, training and mentoring resource which Heather now solely leads and mentors seekers after understanding and new dream interpreters around the globe.

As someone who has now also interpreted many dreams, taught thousands, in several countries on four continents, I highly commend Heather, this book and The Dreamhouse to you all.

Rick Hayes

Founder and Director, Streams Training Centre, North Atlantic Dreams
(www.northatlanticdreams.net)

DREAM JOURNEY

Ever since I was a young girl I would have the following dream on a regular basis, probably at least once a year.

To be honest with you, I had dismissed the dream as one of those 'things' that would simply bug me every once in a while but tried not to pay too much attention to it. Then I happened to be at CLAN Gathering in St Andrews, Scotland (a Christian conference) where a team from Phoenix Vineyard Church in the USA were doing a couple of seminars on dream interpretation. So I went along to the first one simply out of interest. At the end of the seminar they asked for anyone there who had a dream they wanted interpreted, to write it out and hand it in to them and they would see if they got an interpretation. Immediately, this dream came into my mind, very vividly. It seemed so real at the time that simply remembering about the dream brought me out in a cold sweat. I was intrigued by my reaction and why I had suddenly remembered this dream, so I wrote it down and handed it in.

This is what I wrote ……
"In my dream I was allowed to play in the street outside of my home. At the bottom of the street was a factory that had a siren. When the siren went off in my dream I had to run inside to stay

safe from foxes. I heard the siren but for some reason I couldn't get inside the house and had to try to hide from the foxes. I remember being aware of the foxes trying to sniff me out. I called for my Dad to come and help me or find me, but no-one came."

The following day I was surprised when the team said that they had an interpretation for my dream. The interpretation I was given basically said that Satan was using this dream to instill fear in my life. The reason for the fear was to stop me becoming the person God had created me to be.

Something in me just knew that what they said was right. I was constantly afraid that I had to get everything right first time because nobody would ever come to help me as I didn't deserve it …… and so it went on.

That was nearly twenty years ago now and, looking back, I can still see times where the fear, anxiety and insecurities that this dream played on, affected how I lived and viewed my life.

Since then I have taken courses taught by Streams Ministries International (then led by John Paul Jackson) on how to understand dreams using the Biblical, or Ancient Hebraic, method of dream interpretation. Initially I felt that the courses were simply for my information. I had taken the courses – end of story. I didn't think that I could interpret my own dreams, never mind anyone else's. So, at the end of the courses called 'Understanding Dreams and Visions' and 'Advanced Workshop in Dreams and Visions', I shut my notebook, put it on a shelf and didn't look at it again for a long time.

About eighteen months later I was asked to attend an outreach event where I would be part of a team interpreting dreams for university students. My feelings were that I was no good at this but I would go along and make up the team numbers. I had asked if could go out to New Hampshire and do the training to become a teacher for the Art of Hearing God course and saw this as a 'hoop' that I had to jump through to fulfil requirements for teacher training. I planned to sit in with a team and listen and pray – I really didn't think that I would have anything positive to contribute to the dream interpretation process. When I arrived at the event I was surprised to learn that, not only was I to be part of a team, I was to be a team leader. That meant I was responsible for delivering the interpretations to the dreamers. Was I scared? You bet! I thought that the organizer of the event was trying to be funny – there was no way this could be a serious suggestion, but it was. Then I remembered a key component of the method of interpretation I had studied: the interpretation of dreams belong to God, my role was to listen carefully to the spiritual connection that existed between myself and my Heavenly Father. Many of the dreams that were interpreted that night were Destiny Dreams, by that I mean that the dreams contained messages for these young adults specifically about who they were created to be and the destinies that lay before them.

Here is one example - One young man came to our team that night and told us that he had a recurring dream that goes as follows.

In my dream I was crossing a road and was hit by a white truck. I was not hurt and I managed to cross the road. Once I got to the other side I looked back and noticed that the white van would also knock over other people as it drove up and down the street. I would go back into the road and help the people to get to the other side by telling them which way they had to go. What I was surprised at was that no-one was seriously hurt but I wanted to make sure that they were all safe.

The little team I was part of knew that this was a significant dream for this person and we wanted to make sure that we got the interpretation right. We knew that the dream was saying that this young man was being called by God to be an evangelist, what we didn't know was where he was spiritually and what language he would understand. So what we told him was that he was about to encounter something that would make a big impact in his life, he would then explain to other people what a difference this thing could make to their life and how they could find safety. We were thanked for our interpretation and the young man left. About half an hour later he came back into the room and joined the queue for a different team of dream interpreters. At this point, I must admit, my heart sank and I couldn't help but think that we had got the interpretation so wrong that he had come for a second opinion! When he got the chance this young man popped back across to our team and said; "I hope you don't mind, but what you said about my dream felt so good, I'm bringing my friends now to get interpretations for their dreams." My team was blown away – here, within the space of a few minutes, was the interpretation being worked out. He was bringing his friends to a place where they would find spiritual life.

By the time the event finished I was aware that connecting people with the spiritual messages in their dreams was not only something that I could do, but I could deliver correct interpretations, and it was fun!

Since 2005 I have been studying this method of dream interpretation in great depth. During that time I have interpreted somewhere in the region of four thousand dreams in all manner of places: conferences, people's houses, new age fairs, over the internet and so on. In 2011 I became Masters Certified Dream Interpreter and I now have the privilege of teaching other people how to use this method of interpretation and giving talks at events like Holistic Ways Festivals (these are New Age type events that are held in a number of cities throughout Scotland).

I now want to share some of the insights I have gleaned along the way with you. Please remember that this is simply meant to be an introduction to this method of dream interpretation. In no way do I intend that this book will answer all your questions. In fact, my most sincere wish is that by reading this book you are left with a deep hunger to connect with God and understand spiritual dreams for yourself. I cannot recommend the courses that are available from Streams highly enough. If this book piques your interest in the topic of dream interpretation then your next step should be to head over to their website and check out where courses are running live or sign up for an online option.

So, enough about me and my journey – let your adventure into the world of spiritual dreams and the Biblical method of interpretation begin …………

2 DREAMS IN THE SCRIPTURES

When I mention to some Christians that I interpret dreams sometimes I am met with a quizzical look, quickly followed by the question: Is that Biblical? The short answer to that question is: Yes! The Biblical method of dream interpretation has its roots in the Judeo-Christian tradition of spirituality. If you look through the various books of both the Old and New Testament, you can find dreams mentioned almost from start to finish. John Paul Jackson said that approximately one-third of Scripture is connected to either a dream or a vision. There are more verses about dreams than there are about taking communion, but we would never dispute that communion is Biblical. Somewhere along the line there has been a disconnect between dreams and Christianity, especially in Western cultures but this should not be the case. In the next few pages hopefully I will pique your curiosity to find out more about this for yourself.

The book of Genesis is where we find the story of Joseph, who is probably the most well-known dream interpreter of all time. In the account of his life, you can follow his development as a dream interpreter: from a brash youth who didn't seem to think twice about telling his family that he was destined for greater things than them, to a man of wisdom who recognizes that actually understanding the meaning of dreams is a gift that is divinely given to him. He is also interesting because he is one of the few characters that can be found in Scripture that not only interprets dreams of others but we can read about some of his dreams too.

When Joseph first appears in Genesis (chapter 37), he is a young son of one of the Patriarchs, Jacob. Jacob has 10 sons who are older than Joseph and Benjamin who is his younger brother, but Joseph is very obviously the apple of his dad's eye. You can read there that Joseph told his older brothers about a dream he has had where they all had sheaves of corn but the sheaves that belonged to the brothers bowed down to Joseph's sheaf. Then later another dream is recorded – in this dream the sun, moon and eleven stars all bow down to Joseph. It is interesting to note here that although Joseph is the one credited as being a dream interpreter, with these two dreams it is his brothers and father who say what these dreams mean. This says to me that the ability to interpret dreams is not meant to be restricted to the elite few – but more of that later!

If you skip on a few chapters to Genesis Chapter 40 you will come to the part in Joseph's story where he interprets the dreams of his fellow prisoners. (If you feel so inclined, you can read the chapters in between which will give you the background as to what got Joseph to this place.) Instead of the brash young man strutting his 'stuff' in public from Chapter 37, Joseph has now been through a variety of trials and all he would seem to have left in the world is his connection to the one Joseph knows can give the interpretation of dreams - God. Joseph finds himself in a difficult position, he is asked to give the meanings of two dreams, which at first glance, appear to be very similar. Each dream is connected to the job that the dreamer had before they found themselves in prison and the number 3 is significant in both dreams. Fortunately for Pharaoh's cupbearer, he told Joseph his dream first and was informed that the dream meant in three days he would be restored to his former position. Buoyed by this interpretation, the baker told his dream to Joseph. He must have genuinely been crest-fallen when Joseph communicated that the meaning of the dream was that in three days he would die. (Now do you see why I said it was fortunate that the cupbearer went first? If it had been the other way round, I can just imagine the cupbearer denying that he'd ever had a dream!) However, these dreams show us a very important point with regard to Biblical dream interpretation – do not expect that every dream will have a positive interpretation! Sometimes God will use dreams to communicate a very difficult truth about a situation that we may not want to hear.

Genesis Chapter 41 holds the most important phrase that came from Joseph. In verse 16 he declares to Pharoah that he is not able to interpret his dream but that God may grant the interpretation. This was a bold statement to make before the most powerful man on earth at that time. Imagine the scene, Pharoah wants a dream interpreted, he is told Joseph is the man for the job and the first thing that Joesph says is "I can't do it!". How far has he come from the young man who seemed so sure of himself? Now we are confronted with someone who is acutely aware of his limitations but, even in a pressurized situation, is confident in his God. Joseph is now ready for the responsibility that God had created him for – to become Pharoah's right-hand man.

Joseph is one example we have in the Bible for dream interpreter. The other main example we have is Daniel.

In Christian scriptures the book of Daniel is found under the section of the Old Testament that is often referred to as 'prophets'. In the Jewish tradition (or Hebrew Bible) though, Daniel is not classed as a prophet but his book can be found in the section of their scriptures that is referred to as 'writings'. For our purposes here though it does not really matter if Daniel was a prophet or not, both traditions keep the idea that he was a man of great wisdom who was called upon by leaders of nations to interpret their dreams.

In some respects, Daniel is a very different character from Joseph. Daniel from the very start shows a great respect for the spiritual tradition that he was born into. He is careful about what he eats and drinks. He spends time in prayer and meditation on a daily basis and would rather obey his God than the totalitarian rulers of his day. This means that Daniel develops a very close relationship with God. The relationship between the two is such that not only can Daniel receive interpretations to dreams from God, dreams can be revealed to him without the dreamer saying what the dream was! King Nebuchadnezzar used this to find out for himself how 'real' Daniel's abilities are.

Interestingly, none of the dreams mentioned in the book of Daniel are his own. There are visions which are recorded as being had by Daniel, but all the dreams are attributed to other people (namely various rulers of Babylon such as Nebuchadnezzar and Darius). So, unlike Joseph who seemed to be a mix of both dreamer and interpreter, Daniel appears to have been more of an interpreter. (This is kind of like me really, as I have very few dreams of my own to interpret. So I feel as though I am in good company, although I'm not too keen on the lion business!)

Daniel was revered by the main political forces of his day as the person to go to if the situation required great wisdom. Whereas Joseph seemed to be a constant figure in Pharaoh's court, the impression we are given from the accounts of Daniel is that he floated in and out of public life. He was around when the various rulers of Babylon required him but at other times he appears to have faded into the background of life at court.

Daniel and Joseph are the only two figures who appear in the Bible that are renowned as Dream Interpreters. In some ways their lives were quite different but the one main thing that they had in common was that they both had to rely on God for the interpretations of dreams. So what we, in the 21st century, can learn from these ancient characters is that clear channels of communication with God is of vital importance. Repentance and forgiveness in addition to regularly spending time with God is the key – but we'll return to this subject later.

What I don't want you to be doing right now is thinking "Well I'm nothing like Daniel or Joseph so I might as well give up now!" Keep going …

Further investigation of both the New and Old Testaments will show a vast array of other people who had dreams and were able to understand them. I have already mentioned that it seems as though Joseph came from a family of people who could interpret dreams but there are lots of others. Perhaps you will find you are more like one of these people.

Can I encourage you to have another read of the Christmas story in both the gospels of Matthew and of Luke? Have you noticed how many dreams there are there? Joseph (Jesus' earthly father, not the one from the book of Genesis) has at least two that he understands immediately. In the first he is encourgaged not to break off his engagement to Mary. If Joseph hadn't understood this dream and broken off his engagement with Mary, then she would not have had to accompany him to Bethlehem for the census and Jesus would have been born in Nazareth. That was not what was in God's plan for His son. In the second dream Joseph is warned of Herod's plans to kill any children who might potentially be the 'new-born King of the Jews' that he had heard about from the Wise Men. Joseph knew that he should flee with his family to Egypt in order to keep Jesus safe. Again this fulfilled a prophetic word about the Messiah being called out of Egypt.

Also connected to the nativity, one of the Wise Men/Magi/Kings has a dream warning them to return home by a different route so avoiding the need to call in to see Herod again. This meant that they would not reveal the location of the Messiah to the King who wanted this threat to his own position eradicated. Although these are seen as learned or wise men, there is no indication in Scripture that these people had a living faith in God. Yet, one of them had a dream which is recorded in scripture that, undeniably, has come directly from God.

Further on in the story of Jesus' earthly life you can come across a tiny fragment of insight into the life of Pilate's wife. She is only mentioned once (we don't even have her name) but she understands that a dream she has had means that Jesus is innocent and that her husband should have nothing to do with his punishment. Again there is nothing in scripture that indicates she has a personal relationship with God, but He shares truth with her as she sleeps (see Matt 27:19).

It is interesting to note that for Christians the two most significant festivals in the spiritual calendar, Christmas and Easter, have connections with dreams. Jesus' earthly life was book-ended with dreams, perhaps this indicates that dreams are more important than many Christians currently give them credit for.

As you examine all the dreams that are recorded in the Bible (I hope you didn't expect me to list them all here for you), you will find that some are sent to people who are close to God but, as mentioned above, some people have no recognizable connection to God. So what does this tell us? Firstly it could be that there are times when we are so busy during our waking life that the only way God can get our attention is to send us dreams while our body is asleep. Secondly, it shows that God can send dreams to anyone but not everyone has the framework needed to reach the correct interpretation of the messages. As Christians then, this can open the doors to having spiritual conversations or outreach opportunities that may not have been possible before.

I was challenged recently by a teaching from Roy Godwin who was the director of Ffald-y-Brenin in Wales. He was talking about people in Muslim countries who meet Jesus in their dreams and how Christians in the west were praying for more of these encounters for people in closed countries.

One story he told was of a missionary lady who would order a taxi every morning to drive her 30 minutes or so across town to a coffee shop. She would spend the time in the taxi chatting with the driver and eventually would ask him if he had ever had dreams of a man in white. Invariably the driver said that he had. The missionary would then spend the rest of the journey explaining that the driver had dreamed about Jesus and would leave them with some information about how they could find out more. She would then go to the coffee shop, drink her coffee and then order a taxi to take her home again and repeat the conversation she had had on the way there.

Roy then said we are all very good at praying these kind of prayers for people who live far away. His next statement is what brought me up short: Why are we not praying the same thing for the people who live next door? Or our family and friends? Or work colleagues? Of course we should be, but I wasn't then (but I am now!) They are in need of these encounters just as much as much as people in far flung lands.

So now that we've explored a little bit about the background to this method of dream interpretation, let's start dealing with some of the nitty gritty regarding dreams and how you can start working on dreams for yourself.

3 TYPES OF DREAM AND THEIR PURPOSE

Another question that I am often asked by Christians is this: isn't dream interpretation from New Age or occultic activities? Hopefully the previous chapter will have helped to allay some of these fears. However, you will see from the information below that the Biblical method of dream interpretation is very different from some of the other forms of dream analysis that are prevalent in the 'self-help' sections of book shops.

Think about this - have you ever had a dream interpreted but the interpretation didn't seem to satisfy you? One reason for this happening could be that a psychological method of interpretation was used when the dream was spiritual. What do I mean by that? Well, let me explain.

Freud

One of the most common methods of interpreting dreams in the 20th and 21st centuries, 'dream analysis', was developed by Sigmund Freud. His methodology is based on his assumption that all dreams are generated by the dreamer themselves and have no external origins. Freud dismisses any other method of interpreting dreams which allows for the possibility of any force out with the dreamer being able to influence the content of a dream. He has no time for any of the historic beliefs that dreams can be influenced by the spiritual realm, or come from God – such an idea does not fit with his 'scientific' method. However, my reading of his material does not show me great science – his examples of dreams and how he came to the interpretation are mainly based on his own dreams and experiences he knew that he had.

This method of interpreting, or analysing, dreams is based on the assumption that dreams are simply a reflection of how the dreamer wishes things to be. Freud refers to this as 'wish-fulfilment'. If your dreams are anything like some I've had, you will be aware that there are some that would never be referred to as 'the fulfillment of things we wish we had in our life' (we usually call these nightmares). Freud gets round this 'problem' by saying that these dreams are 'in disguise'. By that he means that nightmares may reflect thoughts, ambitions, wishes, that we do not want to acknowledge. Freud's reasoning for this is that nightmares are the product of feelings that would seem impolite or politically incorrect to admit to in the cold light of day, even to ourselves.

He uses an example of one dream he had where he dreamed of a friend who was going for a promotion similar to one that was potential for Freud at that time. This friend appeared in the dream to be Freud's uncle and in a second dream scene had an elongated face and a yellow beard. Freud, when he eventually started to work on an interpretation for this dream, remembered this his uncle, Joseph, had had an elongated face and a yellow beard so the dream must be him equating his friend with his uncle. Uncle Joseph, to Freud, was a simpleton; therefore the dream must be telling him that Freud actually thought of his friend as a simpleton. Now this was not how Freud wanted to think of his friend while he was awake and this was why, so he reasoned, his first response to the dream was that it was all nonsense! Freud then assumed that the dream was telling him that he was bound to get the job as he was so much better than the other candidate.

(It is interesting to note that although Freud says that all dreams have meaning, in the example I have quoted above, Freud says that there was more to the dream but that the second scene of the dream was not important. This is very different from the approach of the Biblical method of dream interpretation as I will show later).

Jung

Another main methodology that is used in society for interpreting dreams is that which was devised by Carl Jung. He was a student of Sigmund Freud's but went his own way. There are aspects of Jung's work which are really useful, such as being the basis for Myers-briggs tests, and this is why much of his teaching has also filtered its way into the church. On the plus side, Jungian approach to dreams does allow for the possibility that dreams can come from sources outwith the dreamer. However, when it comes to interpreting dreams there is a problem, as Jung has drawn together a number of sources from which he then unhelpfully uses to attribute the meanings of symbols in dreams.

Carl Jung draws on mythology and classical symbolism and mixes this with Biblical sounding symbology. A deeper examination of Jung's personal beliefs show that he had a warped sense of who God is that doesn't line up with the God we read of in the Old and New Testaments. If you use Jungian suggestions for what symbols may mean in a dream you might not end up with the true interpretation.[1]

One way you can test the difference that the method used to interpret a dream can make to the end result is simply this – go to any dream in the Bible and then interpret the dream using your chosen method. My practice of this has shown that any method other than the Biblical method means that you end up with a

---

[1] If you are interested in reading more about Freud and Jung and how their dream methods differ from Biblical interpretation I highly recommend that you read "The God of Dreams" by Archie W.N.Roy PhD

different interpretation from the one recorded in the Bible. Personally, I want to be sure that I am using a method that brings me to the same conclusions as scripture – wouldn't you?
So what is the Biblical method of interpretation like? In the rest of this chapter we will start to explore this in more detail.

Biblical Interpretation

The Biblical method of interpreting dreams allows for three different sources for the dreams to have originated from.

The first is similar to Freud's prognosis: some dreams can come from the dreamer themselves. Dreams that come from the dreamer's own psyche (or soul) show things that the dreamer wants to happen i.e. their own wants and desires. One example of this type of dream that I have come across is this:

"I dreamed I was pushing a baby in a pram and I was very happy"

The dreamer was a young lady in her late teens or early twenties. The interpretation that was given to her was very simple – this dream shows your desire to be a mother and that is something you are looking forward to. How did the team get to that conclusion about the dream? Well, none of the symbolic interpretation (that I will talk more about in chapters 4-6) made any sense. In addition to this, none of the team members felt that there was a spiritual interpretation to the dream, any interpretations we came up with simply didn't 'sit right' with our spirits. This dream was a reflection of the dreamer's own hopes and dreams.

Other types of dream which originate within the dreamer can be influenced simply by the state of the dreamer's body. For example, if the dreamer has a fever then they may experience some very strange dreams during this time as their body tries to fight the illness. Women who are pregnant can also have some 'weird' dreams as their bodies adapt to the changes in hormone levels and the fact that they have another person growing inside them. Babies can start to dream two to three months before they are born and it is possible that because of the close links they have with their mother during this time that mums and baby's dreams can combine. Needless to say this produces very strange dreams.

Dreams can also be influenced by a change in the balance of chemicals within our body. You will have heard stories of people having hallucinations after they have taken illegal drugs, but some medication that your doctor prescribes for you can have a similar effect. Some foodstuffs, such as coffee or chocolate, might also influence the content of your dreams as they change chemical levels in your body to enhance your performance, mood and so on. In a way then, the old adage might be true, if you have a weird dream – it could have been the cheese you ate before you went to bed!

In all of the examples that I have mentioned in this section above, there will be no spiritual interpretation for the dream. Any attempt you might make to interpret these dreams will find you tying yourself in knots trying to get an interpretation that makes any sense at all. The reason for this is simply because they are not spiritual dreams.

One other way that you might get a hint that the dream has come from you rather than any spiritual source is by thinking about any colours you might remember from the dream. In the kind of dreams that we have been thinking about above, colours tend to be dull. Imagine you are painting a watercolour of a beach scene on a lovely summer's day and everything is bright and crisp. Then, oh dear, you didn't realize that there was some black paint on your brush when you go to paint the sky and instead of the lovely shade of blue you were expecting, there is a dirty look to it. That's the kind of colour you often get in this type of dreams.

(Sometimes this is referred to as 'muted colours')

The second and third sources of dreams that are talked about in the Biblical method of interpretation both stem from the spiritual realm.

There are some dreams that come from the spiritual realm are commonly referred to as 'nightmares'. It is a term that we are all fairly familiar with but what actually is a nightmare? Well, a nightmare is a dream, that on waking, you are left with a feeling of fear or a sense of foreboding; you may well experience heart palpitations and a need to switch the light on. Nightmares come from a spiritual force that is determined to stop you from becoming the person you were created to be, i.e.the demonic realm.

Here is an example for you to consider:
On one occasion I was interpreting dreams for people at a street market. A young man approached the team and told us the following series of dreams.
"I am always being chased by zombies or some similar creatures, but they have their hoods up so I cannot see them clearly. If these creatures catch me then sometimes they will hold me against a wall by my throat and try to strangle me or at other times they will try to cut off my tongue."

I think you will agree with me that these are not nice dreams. So if you think about what I said about the reasons for nightmares, what do you think these dreams were about? Not sure? Well, let me help you - by cutting out the dreamers tongue or trying to squeeze the breath out of him, these dreams from the demonic realms were trying to stop this young man from speaking. We need out tongues to form words correctly and we need breath to help us to speak out the words we have to say. The other outcome the dreams were trying to produce was to increase the level of fear he had when it came to speaking. As I pondered this dream with God, I saw that this young man had a destiny that involved speaking. The interpretation that we offered was:

"The purpose of these dreams was to make you afraid. To fulfil your destiny, don't let anyone or anything make you too scared to speak – you have words in you that people need to hear."

The young man was blown away by this and went away really encouraged from this short encounter.

One final comment I would like to make about nightmares is that nowhere in either the dream or a straight interpretation will you find any glimmer of hope – this is the main thing that marks nightmares out as different from dreams which come from the other spiritual source: God.

So what are dreams that come from the Throne Room of God like? Firstly, you may be aware of vibrant colours in the dream. Colour is very important to the God, otherwise we would live in greyscale world. Colours will be dealt with in more detail in a separate chapter later on in the book, but for now you should be aware that colours which you remember on waking from your dream could be a clue to help you to understand the dreams meaning.

Secondly, dreams from the God, as mentioned above, will contain hope within it. Whatever the situation that the dream is dealing with there will be something to let you see that things can change and that the outcome is not inevitable. The scriptural basis that backs this up is Romans 8:1 –

"*Therefore, there is now no condemnation for those who are in Christ Jesus*"

The Holy Spirit may convict you of something in a dream but He will never leave you feeling condemned.

Thirdly, and perhaps most importantly, dreams that come from

the heavenly realm have a purpose to them. Some of the main things these dreams can show you are:
1. Who you were created to be, your destiny if you will.
2. Things in your life which are detrimental to your wellbeing and need to be removed.
3. How God views you right now – what the state of your spiritual life is like
4. What other people are going through so that you can understand them better
5. The solution to a problem you are facing
6. Insight into creativity
7. How healing can take place in your life – this could be physical, spiritual or emotional

Let's spend some time looking a bit more closely at each one in turn.

Destiny Dreams:
These dreams show, or can give you insight into, who you are meant to be. They could be about what kind of career you are to pursue or a characteristic that is an important part of your identity.

If you remember back in Chapter 1 to the dreams that Joseph had when he was young, they show his brothers and even his parents bowing before him. If you were to read further on in the book of Genesis then you find Joseph in Egypt and he has been appointed as Pharaoh's right-hand man. With famine going on for years in the homeland of Caanan, Joseph's brothers travelled to Egypt in search of food and ended up bowing before their younger brother in order to achieve their goal. So, what Joseph dreamed came to pass. The dreams about sheaves of corn and the moon and stars showed that Joseph was destined to become a man of power that his family would bow before. This is a great example of a destiny dream.

These dreams are not restricted to Bible-times. I have encountered people at events I have attended who have similar dreams. On one particular occasion, I was at a music festival in the Scottish Highlands and a young woman came to our team and told us about her dream:

"I was on a plane and it came down miles from anywhere, some people were injured and no-one was around who could help them. I found myself being the only one who could treat these people but I didn't really know what I was doing and, if I'm honest, I didn't want to do it. Everyone survived and eventually we were all taken to safety."

We talked to the young woman about how we felt that the dream was about her and how she had the ability within her to heal people. As we talked about it she disclosed that she had started to train as a doctor but had dropped out of university as she felt overwhelmed by the work and the responsibility. One of the team I was with asked her if she thought the dream could be encouraging her that this was what she was created to do? After a time where tears flowed freely, she agreed that deep down she knew that was what she was supposed to be doing. I would love to finish off the story by being able to tell you that she then went back to university and is now a doctor – but I can't! I have not seen this person again since that day and I have no idea what she is doing now. The role of the team was simply to reconnect her to her God-given destiny, the rest is down to her and God.

Destiny dreams are common in young people and also people who are not currently on a path that will lead them to be whom they were created to be.

Cleansing Dreams:
Have you ever dreamed about being on the toilet or in the shower? Sometimes you are on your own, but sometimes it might seem as though the world can see what you are doing and it can mean that you wake up feeling embarrassed!

These dreams, believe it or not, are sent from God to help us. At certain times all of us either witness or experience things which are not good for us to hold on to.

If you consider why we use the toilet or take a shower in our everyday lives, this might help you to understand what is going on with these types of dreams. These processes remove toxins and dirt from our bodies. In a similar way these dreams make us aware that there are issues that could be toxic in our lives that should be removed. These could be the way we feel about certain people, especially if the emotions are negative, like bitterness, hate or jealousy. It could also include ways of thinking that are detrimental to us reaching our destiny, this could include depressive or suicidal thoughts. Sometimes the dreamer may be aware of what needs to go, at other times they may not. This could be because the God is saving the dreamer from any more pain or anguish connected with the issue that is being removed.

You may have noticed that sometimes when you have toilet or shower dreams your activity is not as private as you might wish it to be. This is simply letting you know that other people will be aware of the cleansing process that you are going through. You may feel that this places you in a vulnerable position. However, they may be able to offer help or support to you during this time.

It is not uncommon for people who deal with child abuse as part of their daily work, such as police officers or social workers to experience cleansing dreams on an almost daily basis (even if they are not aware of the dreams). This is so that the images that they have to look at, or statements they need to hear, as part of their work can be removed in order that the images can do no long term psychological damage to the worker.

Spiritual Condition Dreams:

I have interpreted many dreams that have had the purpose of showing the dreamer how God sees them at that particular point in time. These dreams can highlight attitudes or patterns of behavior that you have which God wants to help you to change in order for you to become the person you were created to be.

The dreamer, however, is not always in a place where they can accept the message that the dream is communicating. As an interpreter I have found that the most negative feedback I have received for interpretations is when it has been this kind of dream.

One particular person had a series of scenes in their dreams where they ended up having arguments with a number of people. At first glance the scenes seemed to be unconnected, however as I spent time meditating with Holy Spirit on the dream I became aware of a common thread in each scene – the arguments were based on the dreamer making assumptions. The interpretation that I fed back to the dreamer was along the lines of the following:

"The dream is showing you that there is turmoil going on in relationships in different areas of your life. God is showing you that the cause of the turmoil is assumptions that you make before you find out the truth about situations. You are being encouraged to go to God to seek His help to change these situations."

The feedback I received from the dreamer was uncomplimentary to say the least! I was told that I was as wrong as I could be. All I could do was to apologize to the dreamer. The story continued a few months later when, out of the blue, I received an email from the dreamer – this time they were apologizing to me. It turned out that in fact, my interpretation had been accurate, but, as the dreamer admitted, at the time they were not willing to accept that the problem in their relationships wasn't other people, but them.

Empathy Dreams:

Another kind of dream that you might experience I call empathy dreams. In these dreams you are shown situations that are happening in the lives of other people. You might get insight into pressures that they are under or things that may have happened in the past which makes them act or react in the way that they do today.

So what are you supposed to do with these dreams? Well, you are not expected to go and bare all to the dreamer. As you might pick up from the name of this category, these dreams are to help you have empathy, or understand what the person in the dream is going through.

In the late 1990s I was having some issues with my then boss. We weren't seeing eye to eye about a couple of things and it was really frustrating me. One night God gave me a dream that showed me some things that were going on in her life that I had no idea about. He also showed me that night how He viewed her – a daughter that He loved and cared for, someone who was very special to Him. Was that how I had viewed this woman? No, not at all. By giving me this dream I was then able to view my boss as God saw her. It didn't change the situation completely but it did give me a better understanding of where she was coming from and so I could empathise with her in a way that I couldn't have done before.

Intercession Dreams

Sometimes when you dream you will be watching all the action that takes place and not interacting at all. With theses dreams it is important to pay attention to what is going on with other people. God is often using this type of dream to show you what is happening in someone else's life so that you can pray for them.

There may be a temptation for the dreamer to say to the person the dream was about that they have dreamed about them. This is not something that is recommended on the basis of the dream alone. All God is asking you to do here is simply to pray for the person – nothing more.

If you are an intercessor, or a leader in church or business, then do not be surprised if God gives you more insight into situations via your dreams. You can be shown how to pray for individuals, organisations or nations by your dreams.

Problem Solving Dreams:
Did you know that it is possible for you to receive solutions to problems while you are asleep?

Elias Howe was working on a design for a sewing machine. He was trying to figure out how he could get a machine that would stitch on both sides of the fabric at the same time. While he was asleep he dreamed that he was being chased by canniblas who caught him and put him in a pot. The cannibals kept prodding him with spears to keep him in the pot.

When he woke up Elias thought about the spears that he saw in his dream. He realized that the spears had holes in the tip. This gave Elias the inspiration that he needed so that he could create a machine that would replicate what he had dreamed. He created a needle with the hole in the tip which then allowed his sewing machine design to work more efficiently.

Creative Dreams:
This type of dream can show you a painting you are to paint, a song you are to write and so on. You might remember the image in your mind's eye, or you might waken up remembering the tune. Some examples of this kind of dream are as follows:

* Salvador Dali described his paintings are "hand-painted dream photographs". This suggests that many of the images he created he had seen most vividly while he was asleep. While he was alive, Dali was so well known for allowing dreams to be the basis of his creativity that even the great film-maker, Alfred Hitchcock, asked for Dali's help with the dream sequence in his film, 'Spellbound'.

* Paul McCartney heard the tune for the Beatles hit 'Yesterday' in a dream. He is quoted as saying the following about his experience:

"I woke up with a lovely tune in my head. I thought, 'That's great, I wonder what that is?' There was an upright piano next to me, to the right of the bed by the window. I got out of bed, sat at the piano, found G, found F sharp minor 7th -- and that leads you through then to B to E minor, and finally back to E. It all leads forward logically. I liked the melody a lot, but because I'd dreamed it, I couldn't believe I'd written it. I thought, 'No, I've never written anything like this before.' But I had the tune, which was the most magic thing!"

In a recent television programme I heard Paul McCartney talking about another of the songs that he wrote for the Beatles, 'Let it Be'. He said that he had been struggling about a certain issue. As he slept that night, he said that his mother, Mary, appeared to him in a dream and simply said to him, 'Paul, let it be'. This was not a phrase that Paul would have used himself at the time. So this dream literally became the song:

When I find myself in times of trouble
Mother Mary comes to me
Speaking words of wisdom
Let it be

*Handel is alleged to have received a full download of the Oratorio "Messiah" in a dream and then spent the next three weeks shut away in a room writing out what he had heard. It is said that that is why he completed the manuscript "Soli Deo

Gloria" (or To God be the Glory)

*I have also seen it written that Harriet Beeching Stowe received the concept for her book 'Uncle Tom's Cabin' during a vision that she had in church but I have been unable to confirm this story.

Healing Dreams:

As the name suggests, these dreams can provide healing. This healing could be physical or emotional. I have heard of one person who dreamed that they were cured of an allergy to nuts. Upon awakening they felt an urge to see if the 'dream was true'. Sure enough they found that they could eat nuts without any allergic reaction (please note I would not recommend this!)

Other people have been shown situations in their life when they have been left with feelings of bitterness or guilt towards someone. After waking from the dream, they have reported that either their negative emotions have gone or that they now understand the other person's perspective and are able to forgive them.

Warfare Dreams:

These dreams involve the actions of the enemy trying to attack the dreamer in some way. The purpose of this is to stop the dreamer from fulfilling the destiny God has in store for them.

What can happen in this type of dream is that the dreamers spirit is still active, even though their body is asleep and so the dreamer is effectively fighting back in real time.

Some people are able to do lucid dreaming during a warfare dream. This means that they are aware that they are dreaming but the also know that they can control what is happening in the dream. Effective weapons that people use during this type of dream can vary from the name of Jesus to speaking words of Scripture. It is not uncommon for people to also find themselves wielding swords or other weapons of warfare and would deliberately fight the demonic entities in the dream.

All dreams which come to you from God are designed for your good. In order to understand the interpretation of a dream, a good question which is worth pondering with God is this: "what is its purpose"? Or to put it another way: "God what do you want me to learn from this dream?" If you can answer this, then you possess a key to help you unlock the fuller meaning of the dream. It may be that you will recognise the category of dream, listed above, your dream fits best with. This will then allow you to start working through with God what the message of the dream is.

One other key that can help with understanding the message of the dream is the colours that are contained within it. This is where we turn our attention in the next chapter.

4 WHY COLOURS ARE IMPORTANT

The colours that appear in dreams, as I have already mentioned above, can give you some insight as to what the dream is about and where it has come from. Before I go any further though, I need to make this disclaimer: if you don't remember any colour in your dreams, don't jump to any conclusions, it might just be that colours are not important.

In the Bible, colours are viewed as being important to God. The rainbow was given as a sign that the earth would never be completely flooded again. The rainbow is composed of every hue of colour and could be said to show the importance of colour in understanding the spiritual aspects of life.

The Tabernacle, where the Jews met with God during their time in the desert, had strict instructions for its interior design. Cloth had to be blue, red or purple. The chief priests were to wear a tunic which had twelve different coloured precious and semi-precious stones attached to the front of it. In the Book of Revelation, access to the eternal city is described as being across an emerald sea. Not a blue sea, not a green sea, but an emerald sea. If colours were not important to God then why are there so many details written about them in the Bible?

One way that you can tell if a colour is important to the meaning of a dream is that it is not what you expect it to be. For example, if you dream of grass and it is green then the colour is not important as you would normally expect grass to be green. However, if the grass is purple then that is out of the ordinary and is an indicator that purple is important in this dream. It can be very easy to get side-tracked with colours in dreams that you miss the main message – so be careful!

Colours can have positive or negative meanings if they appear in dreams, so you need to bear this in mind when you are interpreting dreams.

Below is a list of what colours commonly mean in dreams. Some of these meaning have come from the Bible, so if you study them you will find out where the meanings have come from. (I do not intend listing all the places that these meanings can be found – you need to do that work for yourself!) Other meanings are cultural and so if you or the dreamer comes from a different culture then the meanings could be different. In this case you might need to do a bit a research, don't make assumptions.

This is not meant to be an exhaustive or definitive list; it is simply to get you started. So, if none of these suggestions seem to be 'right' in the particular dream you are dealing with then discuss it with God. If you remember back to the story of Joseph in the book of Genesis than you will notice that he asserted that interpretation of dreams belongs to God. As this is the case with interpreting spiritual dreams, God will put meanings on symbols that are 'uncommon'. The reason for this is to keep us dependent on our communication channels to Him remaining open.

Red:
Positive – love, wisdom, passion
Negative – hate

Blue:
Positive – revelation, spiritual communication
Negative – depression, sadness

Green:
Positive – new beginnings
Negative – envy, greed, jealousy

Yellow:
Positive – hope, faith
Negative – fear, cowardice

Purple:
Positive – authority, power
Negative – false authority, stolen power

Orange:
Positive – perseverance
Negative – stubbornness

Brown:
Positive – humility
Negative – humanity

Silver:
Positive – redemption
Negative – ransom

White:
Positive – purity and holiness
Negative – a religious spirit

Black:
Positive – mystery
Negative – evil, despair

Pink:
Positive – attraction, affection, childlikeness
Negative – immaturity, childishness

Scarlet:
Positive – a deep love or passion.
Negative – sin

Gold:
Positive – the presence of the God
Negative - idolatry

Gray:
Positive – wisdom that comes with age
Negative – not clear, indecisive

Colours can also give an indication of the source of the dream. As I mentioned above, God loves colour and so dreams that come from Him will appear in full technicolour. If the dreams are muted in colour (or if the colours seem dirty) then they may have come from you, the dreamer. Thirdly, if the dreams are in black and white then it is likely that the dream will have originated from the demonic realm that has plans to harm the dreamer. These are generalities and you may come across dreams that don't see to fit this 'rule'. If you are in doubt go to God and seek guidance from Him.

5 PEOPLE IN DREAMS

So how often have you been told by someone that they dreamed about you the night before? This is a very common response if you happen to remember someone who appeared in a dream that you've had. However, in my experience, ninety-nine times out of a hundred spiritual dreams are about the dreamer rather than anyone else who appeared in the dream.

As you start to interpret dreams another important question that you need to ask is this: who is the dream about? If you can answer this question you are well on the way to interpreting the dream. The person that the dream is about is the one who the majority of the action of the dream revolves around. Basically if that person was not in the dream then there would be no 'story' to the dream.

Dreams are symbolic and, just like colours in the previous chapter, people in dreams have meanings, but there will be occasions that they can represent themselves. In the next section you will find listed some of the most common reasons why people may be appearing in dreams. The rest of this chapter will be divided into the following sections: the name of the person, the role the person holds in the dreamers life, the job of the person, dead people who appear in dreams and last, but not least, unknown people.

Names

One of the most common reasons a person can appear in dreams is because of their name. Names are very important in the Bible but also in Judeo-Christian cultures. If you look throughout the Scriptures you will find numerous occasions when God either insists that babies are given specific names, or adults have their names changed. For example, in the book of Genesis you can read about Abram (which mean High Father) who had his name changed by God to Abraham which means Father of Nations. There is also Jacob who had his name changed by divine intervention to Israel and now has a country named after him. If you look in some of the books of the prophets you will find accounts of how some of these men were told specifically what to name their children. (Not all the names given were flattering – can you imagine the ridicule that Hosea's son would have faced being called 'Lo-Ammi' by his father as this translates into English as 'not mine'?)

But this is not just a Judaic phenomenon, in the book of the Acts of the Apostles you can read about Saul whose name was changed to Paul in his dramatic spiritual encounter on the Damascus Road and even Jesus, himself, got in on the act by changing Simon's name to Peter. These are just a few examples, if you search throughout the Old and New Testaments you will find others for yourself.

From this we can see that to God, names are important and are used in symbolic ways in our dreams even in the 21st century.

I am not proposing to write out a list of every name that could conceivable be thought of here. However, what I will do is point

you in the direction of a couple of resources that I have found particularly helpful.
1) www.babynames.com – this website is very easy to use, simply type in the name of the person and it will automatically generate the most common meaning for that name (oh and it's free!)
2) The Name Book by Dorothy Astoria – this book gives you the meaning of names and will also point you in the direction of certain Judeo-Christian texts to give you a bit of background to why the name means what it does. (You will find a link to this book on the Dream House website www.thedreamhouse.co)

The choice is yours really, depending on how much depth you want to go into researching the meaning of names. There are lots of books and websites that will give you similar information but after being involved in interpreting dreams for over ten years, these are the two I have found most useful.

When it comes to using someone's name as part of an interpretation to a dream you need to apply the meaning. For example if the person in the dream is called Ann, then the meaning of the name is 'grace'. So if the dream involves Ann giving something to the dreamer, then the interpretation could be about the dreamer receiving the grace they need to be able to handle a situation well.

Role

Another reason people can appear in dreams is because of the role that they play in the dreamer's life.
Here are some examples of what people can symbolize in dreams.
- **Mother**: can represent the person's spiritual community or church. This is borne out by the original meaning of Mother's Day, or Mothering Sunday, when people were

allowed to leave the places that they worked and return home to their 'mother church'. Another version of the origins of the phrase lead us to the same conclusion: people could go to see their mother and attend their home church on Mother's Day.

- **Mother-in-law**: an issue of legalism within the person's spiritual community. It might reveal an attitude of things having to be done to the letter of the law rather than out of love.
- **Father:** depending on the kind of relationship the dreamer had with their own father, fathers appearing in dreams could represent God. In the Lord's Prayer, Jesus tells his disciples to pray to their 'Heavenly Father'. In John 14 Jesus also tells his disciples that if you have seen me, you have seen the Father. So the symbology here is clear. If however the dreamer had a bad relationship with their earthly father then there are issues here. It would be unusual for a loving Heavenly Father to use such negative symbolism to portay Himself in a dream, but He might do this if the purpose of the dream is to bring healing.
- **The dreamer's child/children:** something that the dreamer is responsible for. If it's someone else's offspring it could mean that the dreamer is taking on responsibilities that should be borne by other people.
- **Boss:** someone who has authority in the dreamer's life (could also be used to symbolize God)
- **Friend:** someone who will stand by the dreamer or listen to them in times of need.
- **Spouse/partner:** someone that the dreamer is intimately involved with. Spiritually this could refer to Jesus. In Reveletaion Jesus is talked about as the Bridegroom waiting for His Bride (the Church) and we get similar imagery from the Song of Songs.

Job

A person can also appear in a dream because of the job they do or the profession that they represent rather than themselves.

In the book of Judges chapter 7, you will find the story of a man called Gideon. He was given the task of leading the Jewish people into battle against the Midianites and, naturally, he was scared. God told him to creep into the enemy camp one night. While he was there, Gideon overheard some of the Midianite soldiers talking about a dream where a roll of bread came through their camp and destroyed everything – the Midianites knew that the bread roll represented Gideon and that he was going to destroy them. How did they know that the bread was Gideon? Well, earlier in the book you can read about Gideon treading grain, his family were involved in making flour which is the key ingredient of bread. So for the Midianite soldiers, Gideon's family business helped them to understand what the dream meant.

Below are some suggestions for what a person's job could mean if they appear in a dream.

- **Police officer:** someone who has the right to stop the dreamer going in the wrong direction or who has the authority to question their actions.
- **Head of State**: God - ultimate authority
- **Doctor/Nurse**: someone who can bring healing to the situation
- **Teacher**: someone who can educate the dreamer about what is going on.
- **Farmer**: someone who provides your spiritual food (teaching)
- **Soldier**: someone with the job of protecting the dreamer.
- **Actor**: someone who is not really who they are pretending to be/playing a role

Dead People

A number of people at various events have asked me why people that they know are dead have appeared in their dreams. There can be a few reasons for this.

Firstly, as I have said before dreams are often symbolic. Dreaming about members of your family who have died can by symbolic of things that have passed down your family line. These could be positive things that you need to hold on to, or an invitation to break a negative cycle of behaviour.

Secondly, dead people appearing in your dreams can be a natural part of the grieving process. The dreams can show how well, or otherwise, you are coping with their death.

At one event a teenage girl came with a series of dreams where she kept seeing her grandmother who had died. The dreams all showed the girl hurrying to help her grandmother in a variety of situations. Initially I couldn't understand what the dreams were about so I took a few moments and listened for God to give me some guidance. I became aware of one word "guilt", so I asked the girl if she felt bad about her grandmother dying. At this point she started to cry. It turned out that on the day her grandmother died, the girl had persuaded her mum to go shopping with her rather than visiting her grandmother. The girl was racked with guilt that her grandmother would still be alive if she hadn't gone shopping. We were then able to talk openly with her about her need to forgive herself – it really wasn't her fault. We then encouraged her to connect with God and ask for help to deal with her grandmother's death in a healthy manner.

On another occasion a young man told of a series of dreams where a friend of his kept turning up. In real-life, the dreamer and his friend had been involved in a crash – he survived but his friend had been killed. The first dream was centred on the crash and its aftermath but the series of dreams progressed until one that the dreamer had had just a couple of nights before we met. In this dream the friend had caught their jacket on a barbed wire fence and the young man was trying to help them get free. Eventually the friend took the jacket off, left it attached to the fence and walked off, leaving the dreamer at the fence. After the friend had walked a few steps, they turned to look back at the dreamer, waved, and then kept on walking. I was able to encourage this young man that the series of dreams were a reflection of his grieving process. The last dream showed that he was being let 'off the hook' and that he was finally able to let his friend go. There was to be no guilt about why he had survived and his friend had not. The relief in the young man's body language was tangible and there was a sense of closure to the situation.

Unknown people

People who appear in your dream sometimes feel very familiar but you never quite see their faces or be fully aware of who they are. Often these people represent spiritual beings. If these unknown people are being helpful in the dream then they will often represent angels, unknown people who are being hindrances in the dream will often be demonic spirits.

6 OTHER SYMBOLS

As I have already mentioned, the spiritual understanding of dreams requires an understanding that dreams are full of symbols. The Bible also contains symbols. The Psalms and Song of Solomon are examples where metaphors and symbolism are used to great effect and it is up to the reader to try to understand what the symbolism means. In the gospels there are numerous parables that are told by Jesus to various groups of people. The difference with these parables compared to the Old Testament passages is that they record later conversations Jesus had with his disciples where he explained what the parables mean. Therefore, we can have insight into what these particular symbols are meant to represent. So a great place to start gaining an understanding what symbols in dreams could mean is to study the symbols in these Biblical books. The way God communicated with people in Scripture is similar to how communication takes places today.

What you will find if you go through these scriptures is that there are some symbols which are given more than one meaning. For example in the parables that he told, Jesus uses the symbol of 'seed'. However, in one parable he tells his disciples that the seed represents faith, in another story he uses seeds to represent the spiritual kingdom. From this you can see that there is no quick fix or easy right answer to what symbols in dreams mean. In order to understand spiritual dreams, we need to rely on help from the

God, just as Joseph did back in Genesis 41, to know which meaning to attribute to each symbol that appears in dreams. This is why you are very unlikely to see a definitive dream dictionary produced for this method of dream interpretation.

Despite my saying this, I can hear the questions you are asking – a lot of things that appear in your dreams didn't exist when these ancient texts were written, so how do you go about trying to interpret them? Well the simplest answer I can give you at this stage is that you meditate on how the object is used. For example a phone is used as a tool for communicating and, most of the time; you cannot see the person on the other end of the call. Therefore, a phone could symbolize communicating with the spiritual realm (otherwise referred to as prayer!)

In this next section I will give you some general principles for interpreting symbols – but remember these are simply the most common meaning for these symbols that I have come across over the years but not necessarily the only meanings these symbols can ever have. AS you explore this method of communication from God I am sure you will come up with many other possibilities.

Buildings

The easiest example that I can give you is this. One of the parables that Jesus told his followers was about 2 builders (see Matt 7:24-27). One built a house on solid ground with good foundations and the other built his on sand; when the storms arrived, the house on the sand fell down. When Jesus explained this parable to his disciples he told them that the house represented the builder's life. So, if you dream about something happening in your house, in the Biblical method of dream interpretation, then you are often dreaming about something that is happening in your life.

There can then be subtle nuances about which room in your house you are in.

The **kitchen** is where you prepare food. There are examples in both the Old and New Testaments where spiritual teaching is symbolized by items such as bread, so this could be indicating that you are preparing to teach or share a spiritual message with other people.

The **dining room** is where you eat food – so this could be about the spiritual teaching you are currently taking in.

The **bedroom** – this could be about you needing to rest or maybe showing you how intimate you are with God at that time in your life. The Song of Solomon in the Old Testament has many examples of this kind of symbolism.

The **attic/loft**, well this is where we store things that we don't necessarily need anymore but for sentimental reasons perhaps we don't want to throw out – so dreaming about this could be showing you something from your past or memories.

The **toilet** – as mentioned in a previous chapter, dreaming of being in the toilet is to do with cleansing, a spiritual detox if you will.

This can be extrapolated out to other forms of building and situations in the following manner:

School – a place to go to be educated. Pay attention to where you are in the dream; are you a student or the teacher? Is there something that God would like you to learn from the situation or are you there to give instruction to other people?

Hospital – a place to go for healing (this could be physical, emotional or spiritual healing depending on the context of the dream) Again, what is your role in the dream? Are you a patient or are you part of a healing profession (doctor, nurse etc.). This could help you to work out if you have a healing ministry or if there is an area of your life that rquires healing.

Restaurant – this is similar to a dining room, but more people go there to eat, so it could be talking about your spiritual community and what you are being taught when you are together. Also, when you eat at a restraurant there is usually a cost to pay for what you receive but in a dining room, if the meal has been prepared by family or friends then it is more likely to be free.

Hotel – are you there on business or pleasure? Whichever it is, you do not stay at a hotel for very long so this dream is about a time in your life that has a limited duration.

Corridor/Hallway – you are usually going from one place to another, so this would symbolize a time of change or transition.

I hope that by now you are starting to see the pattern of how this works and will be able to apply this to your own dreams.

Just a note about timings – if the setting looks historic, it could be about your (or your family's) past. For example, you could dream about the house you grew up in, but in the dream you are the age you are now – this dream is likely to be about something from your childhood that is affecting how you live your life now. Conversely, if things look 'space-age' then it could be about the future. If things look 'normal' then it could be about now!

Numbers

If you look at the Bible you will find that numbers appear on many different occasions. Like everything else I have mentioned so far, numbers also have symbolic values that can influence what they mean in dreams. For example, when talking about forgiveness Jesus said that he expected his disciples to forgive someone 70x7. Did he mean that people were to forgive someone 490 times and that on the 491 they were to remain unforgiven?

(Jewish law at the time gave the expectation that you had to forgive someone 7 times). No, in this instance the figure is symbolic of continually forgiving someone, or not holding a grudge against them. You will find numbers throughout all the Bible: but beware the book of Numbers that is attributed to Moses – it reads just like a very long list!

I have seen dreams where the numbers on a digital clock have referred to chapters and verses of books in either the Old or New Testament. Without direction from God, all I can suggest you do with these is to look at every corresponding verse until you come across one that 'fits' with the rest of the dream.

In the Jewish faith there is a tradition of assigning numbers to letters. You might be of the opinion that you have never come across this before; however I am willing to bet that you have heard the phrase "666 is the number of the beast"! This is where this phrase has come from. The combined total of the numbers associated with the Giver of Dreams' enemy is 666. I don't claim to understand this completely and so, if you are interested in finding out more about this I would recommend that you look at Jerry Lucas and Del Washburn's book 'Theomatics'.

On an easier level, here are some numbers and what they represent in the Bible:

1 – God, there is 1 true God.
3 – the Trininy. Father, Son and Holy Spirit
7 – perfection or completion. According to the Book of Genesis, God created the world in 6 days and rested on day 7 because the work was complete.
8 – new beginnings/new start. Day number eight was the start of the second week.
30 – the start of fulfilling your destiny. This is how old Jesus was when he started his preaching and teaching.
40 – a generation. In the Jewish tradition are 40 years

attributed to each generation.

Body Parts

It has been known for people to dream and see parts of their body in different proportions than they are in real life. In terms of the spiritual message that these types of dreams contain there are clues in the Bible.

Thigh - In the book of Genesis you can read the account of Abraham sending his servant to look for a wife for his son, Isaac. In order to confirm the faith Abraham had placed in his servant, the servant had to place his hand under Abraham's thigh (see Genesis 24:2). So, if you dream about having enormous thighs it could mean that you have great faith. Or if your thighs are tiny then it could mean you have very little faith in that instance.

Nose - Another method that you can use to discover what the meaning of a body part is in a dream is to think about colloquialisms. Imagine you dream about someone having a very big nose. It is common to talk about "something smelling fishy" – meaning that something doesn't seem quite right. Therefore, the nose in this dream could mean that the person has a great awareness of when things are wrong. This is often referred to as 'discernment'.

Legs/feet – In common with other methods of understanding symbols, you can also consider what the body part is used for. Legs and feet are our mode of getting from one place to another – a journey. If they were highlighted in a dream as being important, then the dream could be about your spiritual journey, some people refer to this as their spiritual walk.

Eyes – In dreams eyes can show you that your ability to see things in the spiritual realm.

Ears – dreaming of having ears the size of Dumbo the elephant could indicate that you have a great ability to receive spiritual messages.

Teeth – the ancient Hebrews first recorded their holy texts in a form that we would recognize more as pictures than words. In this method of recording there was one 'word' that looked like a tooth and translated from ancient Hebrew into modern day English it means 'Wisdom'. So anyone who is dreaming about their teeth falling out (which is surprisingly common) could be worried about lacking wisdom in a certain situation.

Animals

Throughout the scriptures there are many references to animals that are symbolic. For example the Messiah that the Jewish people were waiting for is described as both a Lamb and a Lion. There are references in the parables to followers of Jesus being likened to sheep and in the Old Testament there's even a story about a donkey who could deliver spiritual messages (see Numbers 22:21-39)!

In addition to what you will find in the scriptures, there are some other methods of seeking meaning for animal symbols that have not been mentioned so far.

Dogs – there is a saying that a dog is 'man's best friend'. So it is quite common for a dog in a dream to represent a friend. However, this depends on what the dreamer's experience of dogs is. For example if the dreamer is afraid of dogs then a dog appearing in their dream could represent an issue that they are fearful of. Another issue you can bear in mind is this: what culture does the dreamer come from? Although I have mentioned that dogs are man's best friend, that is mainly in western cultures, in some eastern cultures dogs are a source of food.

Lions – As I mentioned above, lions are used frequently as symbols in Judeo-Christian scriptures but they can also be used to highlight another way to interpret symbols. If you see a group of lions in a dream – think about the collective noun for a group of lions: pride. So, a group of lions in a dream can represent that characteristic.

I know that there are lots of other areas that could be covered in this chapter: transport, clothing, household objects and so on. However, with the areas that I have covered I think I have given you enough pointers to start seeing the possibilities yourself. (These topics are covered in detail in the Understanding Dreams and Visions course from Streams Ministries www.streamsministries.com) The key to this form of dream interpretation is to remember what Joseph said in Genesis – interpretation belongs to the God, you need to have your communication channels open and clear to be able to receive the information about meaning of the dream from Him.

7 REMEMBERING YOUR DREAMS

So far we have talked about how you would go about interpreting dreams, but before this book is finished it is important that we cover this topic: how do you remember your own dreams?

Firstly it is important that you value the dreams that you have. Our brains are wired in such a way that we can train it to remember things that are important and to forget things which are not. If you are interested in finding out more about this then I suggest that you google 'reticular activating system' and search for websites that will tell you about the filter that our brains have in place. In Western cultures many of us are brought up with the Greek/logic worldview and dreams fall in to the category of 'not logical'. Therefore in relation to dreams it means that if you do not see dreams as important then your brain simply will not remember the dreams that you have. (The Art of Hearing God course from Streams ministries would be good to take if you want to learn more as this topic is mentioned there). You might be saying that you don't dream. However, scientists are fairly sure that the majority of people dream every night and this appears to be important for them to retain good mental health. So there is a distinct difference between not dreaming and not remembering your dreams.

Secondly, before you go to sleep, you should connect with God and ask for help to remember any dreams that you are sent from Him during the night. Some people also find it useful to ask God for help to block any dreams which come from the enemy that are out to harm them (you might refer to this kind of dream as a nightmare).

Thirdly, you can tell your body that you want to waken as soon as a dream ends. If you can do this you are more likely to remember the dream. You might think this is a strange thing to do, but how often have you gone to bed thinking something like "I need to get up at 6.30am" and then find that you waken at 6.29 just before your alarm goes off? This is the same principle: you are in control of your body and you can tell yourself when you want to waken up.

Fourthly, have some method of recording the dream by your bed. Some people use a paper and pen to write down as much as they can remember of the dream and then go back to sleep. Other people have their phone or a recording device there so that they simply speak what they remember and then can go back over everything later. There are some draw backs that you need to be aware of, especially if you share the room with someone else! If the light isn't very bright or if you write everything very quickly so as not to disturb the other person than you might find that your writing is illegible. Similarly with recording if you keep your voice very quiet then when you play it back you might just get an indecipherable mumble!

It can be useful, once you are up and awake, to spend some time going back over the dream and meditate on it with help from God. Depending on your individual preferences, you could:
- write it out again as a story
- record the date thatyou had the dream
- draw a picture of how the dream works out
- pick out the main action points from the dream

- do absolutely anything else with the dream you feel led to do – it is your dream after all

If you do not get an interpretation straight away that feels 'right' for you, I would encourage you not to panic. There could be many reasons for this including: timing (it's not the right time for you to get the interpretation) and partnership (maybe it was your role to receive the message but perhaps it has to be interpreted by someone else).

Keep your dreams somewhere safe and any that you do not have interpretations for, keep going back to them occasionally to see if you have any more clarity about the messages they contain. It can be important for dreamers to 'keep their dream alive'. Even though a dream might have been sitting on the shelf (so to speak) for a number of weeks, months or even years it does not mean that you will never understand what it is about. As you go back over the dream you never know when you will suddenly remember a vital part that you hadn't recorded and this is actually the key to unlocking the interpretation!

If you don't value what you have been given then God may simply stop communicating with you in this way and your spiritual life and development will be the poorer for it. So I would encourage you to grasp what you have been given and work to understand the meaning – but don't forget to ask God for help! If you start trying to interpret spiritual dreams all by yourself you will find that the interpretations you come up with will not satisfy. The dreams you are sent will become like an itch you cannot reach to scratch. Getting a spiritual interpretation for a spiritual dream, on the other hand, brings with it a great sense of peace and relief.

8 COMMON DREAMS

There are some dreams which many people have or variations thereof. In this short chapter I would like to offer you some simple interpretations of what these dreams might mean.

Falling – how often have you dreamed of falling off a building or a kerb? These kinds of dreams are showing the dreamer that there is an area of their life where they are feeling like they are out of control. If in the dream you do not fall to the ground, the message is likely to be that whatever the issue is that you have that is out of your control, it is not going to damage you greatly.

Flying – if you have the ability to fly in your dreams (by this I am talking about flying without the aid of any machines or equipment – kind of like Superman/Superwoman/Superted) then this shows you have the ability to move in the spiritual realm.

Being chased – it is quite common for people to dream that they are being chased by zombies, monsters, werewolves etc. This type of dream indicates that enemies of the dreamer are attempting to stop the dreamer fulfilling their destiny. As I mentioned in an earlier chapter, I once interpreted a series of dreams for a teenage boy who dreamed that he was being chased by zombies and if he was caught the zombies would either cut off his tongue or try to strangle him.

If however, you are being pursued by someone who doesn't make you feel scared but maybe just curious about why they are after you; this could indicate that God wants to develop the communication channels of prayer and intimacy with you.

Losing teeth – you might be surprised how many people have dreams like this! As mentioned in a previous chapter teeth can be connected with wisdom, so losing teeth would mean that you are concerned that you are not being wise about a situation. However you might be able to narrow things down even further. For example, if it is your eye tooth that falls out it might mean that you cannot see the situation clearly and so on.

Snakes – if you think about a snake, it is basically one long tail – another way to describe a tail (or tale) is a story or a lie. So if you dream about being surrounded by snakes then the dream is showing you that your life is surrounded by lies. Depending on the type of snake in the dream then the lies could be trying to poison other people against you (or poison your own mind), or alternatively the lies could be trying to crush you. If you read the story of Adam and Eve in the book of Genesis you will see that the devil is referred to as both Liar and Deceiver so this is not good. However, depending on what happening elsewhere in the dream, snakes can be positive. For a Biblical example of this see the story of Moses in Numbers 21:4-9 This has been used as the emblem for the British Medical Association and would therefore refer to healing.

Taking an exam – if you dream about being back in school taking a test or an exam then the message from the dream could be that there is a lesson which you should have learned in the past but for some reason didn't, you are being given the opportunity to learn that lesson now.

Being naked – most of us, at some time or another, will dream about being naked in public. The natural reaction is to feel embarrassed at this prospect. However these dreams are a message about your character. They show that you are willing to show your vulnerability or transparency to other people. It can also be sending a message to others that with you 'what they see is what they get'. So, rather than being a dream to be ashamed of, these dreams reflect who you really are.

Dreams about ex-partners – dreams like this can be very disconcerting, especially if in the waking world you have moved on and are now with someone else. Most of the time, however, these dreams are to show you that you are being attracted back to something from your past. That could be an addiction or habit of behaviour that was detrimental to you and the dream is warning you that you are heading back down the same path.

9 WHEN IS A DREAM NOT A DREAM?

In western cultures we assume that everything that happens to us while we are asleep is a dream. However, the Biblical method of dream interpretation is not based in western culture and so it opens up other possibilities. There are many spiritual experiences that can happen while we are asleep.

Visions – the Jews differentiated between dreams and visions. For them, dreams need to be interpreted but visions are literal and so require no interpretation. Therefore it is possible to dream while you are awake and have a vision while you sleep! An example of this can be found in the Acts of the Apostles when it is recorded that Paul had a dream where a man appeared to him and called Paul to go to Macedonia. The interpretation of this is that Paul had to go to Macedonia – simple!

Visits to Heaven – dreams can be spiritual experiences where our spirits can leave our physical bodies and go on adventures. I once interpreted a dream for a young woman who said that when she was four, she dreamed that she was taken to a place where there was a large pillar of white light that had gold specks in it. On the other side of the light was a person who simply said to her "this is God". I could not offer the young woman an interpretation for this dream as it was not a dream. All I could say was that when she was four, she was taken to heaven and introduced to God. The sense of relief from the young woman was tangible. She had had many such experiences as she grew up but whenever she tried to talk to someone about it she was dismissed. Finally she had found someone who would validate what had happened to her.

Angelic visitations – Angels and other spiritual beings can visit us during our waking and our sleeping hours. Studying both the Old and New Testaments will show that angels are sent to help us and will often contain messages for us.

If you read through scripture for yourself, especially parts that tell of the Prophets in the Old Testament, you will find many 'strange experiences'. If God could do these things with His people in the past, what could be stopping Him doing the same with His people today? Ezekiel was spun by his hair in mid air during a meeting with the elders

For a dream interpreter using the spiritual method of dream interpretation, it is important not only to be able to give people interpretations for their dreams, but also to be able to help them understand the spiritual experiences that may have happened to them while they were asleep.

10. DREAM INTERPRETATION AS AN EVANGELISTIC TOOL

Since I started seriously studying dream interpretation back in 2005 I have had the priviledge of being part of teams going to various events to interpret dreams. Some of these events have been Christian but some have not. I have been astounded at the goodness of God when He pours out His love for people who are not yet in the Kingdom by giving them dreams.

The purpose of this chapter is simply to share some of my favourite stories with you and hopefully give you some insight into how God is working in the lives of these people.

Refugee –
This is the story of an encounter that my friend Philip had and he gave me permission to share it:
One night Philip and his friends were walking in the city he lives in looking for people to share words of knowledge/prophesy with. They came across a young man on his phone and looking quite sad. They approached him and asked if he was ok. The young man explained that he was a Muslim refugee from the middle-east and had only arrived in the city recently and knew no-one there but this day was his 30th birthday.

Philip and his friends took this young man for dinner in a local restraurant; the waitresses sang 'Happy Birthday' to him and brought him cake. Philip then spoke to the young man and said that it was his birthday so he had to make a wish before he had cake: what would he wish for? Philip was surprised at the response.

"I want to dream of the man in white and change my life".

Philip was curious and asked for more info. This was what the man said:

"Back home I was studying for a Masters degree and my friend met the man in white in his dreams. There was a dramatic change in his lfe after this dream and I want that too!"

Philip and his friends prayed for the refugee that he would indeed meet this man in white. Then they all went their separate ways.

A few months later Philip was at a Bethel conference in another city and who should he meet but the refugee! He was now a Christian.

Sleep –

At an event in London a mother and daughter (let's call her 'Zoe' and she was about 12 years old) came and sat down with the team I was part of.

The mother told us her dream and the team then gave a short interpretation for the dream by my eyes were fixed on the daughter. She was getting more uncomfortable in the situation and the colour was draining from her face. Eventually I asked if she was ok? Her mum replied that Zoe hadn't slept for days. Zoe said that she was too scared to sleep, so I asked her quite quietly if she cold tell me whyat was making her scared. Zoe disclosed that she saw faces when she closed her eyes and heard voices that said nasty things to her.

All I can explain about what happened next is that I felt a holy anger rise within me about what Satan and the demonic realm were doing to this young girl.

I asked Zoe is she had ever heard the name 'Jesus' and she said that she had so I explained that for situations like this 'Jesus' has the most power to help. I then gained Zoe's permission to pray on her behalf. I found myself for the next 10-15 minutes standing in the gap for Zoe, well actually I was kneeling on the floor at her feet. To be honest, I cannot remember all that I said but I know that I started off by removing the hold that demons had over her and then I replaced all the lies that had been spoken to her. Phrases like "you deserve to have friends", "you can be loved", "you are a good girl", flowed from my mouth. Zoe simply sat there with wide eyes and seemed to take in everything that was being said.

After I returned to my seat I asked Zoe if she was ok and she said said yes she was. Then she got up with her mum and left. This is where I genuinely expected this story to stop bt God had other ideas.

A few days later one of the other people that had been on the small team ministering to Zoe and her mum happened to meet 'mum' in the street in London. Yes in a city that has millions of people living and working in it they bumped into each other. Mum was asked how Zoe was doing and her reply astounded the whole team once we heard – Zoe had slept soundly every night since we had ministered to her. She no longer had anything to fear.

I wish I could share a formula with you and explain how all of this worked but I can't because I don't exactly know. What I do know is that I was willing to put myself in the place that God wanted me to be and to follow His promptings. Everything else is down to Him. I am simply humbled to have been the vessel that was used on this occasion.

Sleep Paralysis –

For a couple of years I took a Dream House stand at events called 'Holistic Ways'. These are New Age Fairs that take place in venues throughout Scotland. I found quite quickly that I had favour from the organisers – they would give me space in prime locations for example. I was eventually asked if I would like to give talks at the events. This seemed to be too good an opportunity to miss so I said yes.

The topic I chose was "When is a dream not a dream?" Each timeslot lasted an hour. I spent about 40 minutes talking about translations, visitations, visions and so on. The last 20 minutes was given over to Q+A.

On one occasion I was asked what my views were on sleep paralysis. I wasn't too sure how to answer this (as I must admit sleep paralysis was not a term I had encountered up to this point) so I aked what the person meant by this. She went on to explain that sometimes she wakens up to feel a heavy weight on her chest, or she sees evil hideous faces in her room. Basically she was describing demonic attacks. For my part, there then followed a series of 'arrow prayers' sounding very much like 'Oh God , Oh God, Oh God'. I had no idea what to say!

So, in order to stall a bit, I asked the other people in the room (there must have been about 35 in total) if they had ever had anything similar. About 20 people raised their hands and one person specifically asked me what I would recommend to make these experiences stop! My honest answer was that I didn't know. However, out of my mouth I heard these words: "I believe that names have power and in situations like this, the most powerful name that I am aware of is Jesus".

The thoughts that then ran through my head were 'Oh no, that's my cover blown! Everyone here now knows that I'm a Christian. I'll never be allowed back...' But what happened next still astounds me.

Over to my left a young woman piped up "Yeah, that's right, the name Jesus really works." I then asked her to explain her story.

"One night I woke up and was unable to move. I couldn't roll over. I couldn't talk or get my boyfriend's attention in any way. All I could do was think. Eventually, in my head, I said 'Jesus'. As soon as I said that everything changed. I could move and talk."

My advice to the rest of the people was simple then – just do what she said, it works!

This was definetly an example of the spirit of testimony pointing people to Jesus.

People from other religious backgrounds –

The dream below was sent to the Dream House for interpretation. My initial response was that it was a 'straight-forward' spiritual warfare dream where the enemy was trying to attack the dreamer and stop them from achieving their God-given goals. Then I get to the last sentence – what is your reaction?

In my dream, it began this way that I was lying in bed watching a video where a woman was telling about how her husband/brother (Don't Remember Exactly) shot himself in the mouth while investigating something (D.R.E). I clearly remember that video was not sharable, because it said it can cause some harm or something to the viewer. So I'm into sleep, and I'm hearing noises, I'm hearing whispers and feeling a ghostly presence around me, they want to take me. They're definitely evil and then they take me to a place which appears to be a sort of dungeon where there two floors and two doors, one is for Satan's World and one is for God's world. They're whispering and I can hear it "He is Satan's son, take him" and I'm trying reallllly hard to call out to God, that I need your help, you're stronger. And while I'm picturing God in my thoughts I'm getting hindered by flash images of Nude Women, and making me feel sexually active and I'm loosing my thoughts of Jesus but then I held on and kept reciting his name and then some woman took me from this "Satan's door" to the other door which I believe was "God's door" while the evil ones are chattering "Stop him, don't let him go, stop him"

The moment I enter the door I wake up from this dream, and I realize that it was a dream and I'm actually investigating some sort of high profile murder or suicide (D.R.E) which is somehow connected to spirituality.

Now I wake up from this dream, to a scene where I'm in bed and it's early morning and I go out and find one of the comedians Kapil Sharma and world class cricketer Virat Kohli together and I go for a walk with them. Then Virat starts running and I start chasing him to full strength. Of course I couldn't but there is a speedometer which is measuring my speed and it was close to Virat's speed. After the sprint, he says he's really doing good.

And I feel confident about myself.

And I'm not even a Christian, I'm a Hindu. It's the third dream in past 2 years and the timing is also 3-4 am wherein I have seen evil or demonic dreams. Whenever I start or begin to change my lifestyle or discipline my life, a dream like this definitely comes.

This is the interpretation I sent back:
The dream you had is showing you that there is a spiritual battle going on for your destiny. The videos you have been watching before you go to sleep are allowing images into your spirit which means that Satan and his demons can control many aspects of your life.

You are aware that Jesus is stranger than Satan but Satan is constantly trying to distract you from focusing more on Jesus and how being closer to Jesus could change your life.

In the next dream it would seem that the high profile murder/suicide that you are investigating is the death of Jesus. You need to investigate this for yourself and come to your own conclusions.

The third dream is encouraging you to keep meditating. There will be 2 influential figures who come into your life to help you. Your spiritual life if better than you give yourself credit for. Your spiritual life will develop and grow quickly and you will find this a fun time where you experience much joy.

You may have noticied here that I haven't jumped in with a full biblical exegesis of who Jesus is and why the dreamer should become a Christian. What I did use is some of the language that the dreamer used both in the dream and in additional information that they sent in their email.

What I hope this dream will stir in you is a desire to interact with people of different faith or religious backgrounds from yourself. God is talking to them in dreams and they are having significant spiritual encounters. Some of them need people like you to give some context to these experiences. We hear lots of reports of Muslims meeting the 'man in white' in their dreams (see the example at the end of chapter 2), but people from other faiths are having similar dreams.

Taking one for the team!
On one occasion I was invited to attend a local radio station and interpret dreams live on air. People who listened to the radio show were asked to send in their dreams and myself, and a friend who was with me, interpreted these dream as part of the show. Just as we were about to go into a break the presenter of the show said that she had a dream. During the break the presenter told me about the dream – she was on a chess board and while she made her way across the first few rows on the board everything was bright, light and felt happy as she crossed the midway point though everything changed. The board became unstable, all the colours drained away and that she was in danger of falling off the board. There was more to the dream than this but it is prudent not to put that in print.

As I was sitting in the radio station I was very aware that this dream was showing abuse that the presenter had experienced in childhood. Now I was in a quandry – I instinctively knew that sharing the interpretation live on air was not the best thing to do. As an interpreter one of my values is to always be kind and respectful to the person who has entrusted me with their dream. So, I took one for the team. What I mean by that is this: live on air I said that I didn't have an interpretation for that particular dream. Was that true? No. Was it kind? Absolutely. I had no idea how many people were listening to the broadcast or even who was listening. I certainly felt talking about abuse live on air was the most compassionate option I had for the presenter who had no idea what idea what they had shared with me. The actions that I took were to say to the presenter that I would continue to think about/meditate about the dream over the course of the weekend. On the Monday I sent an email to the presenter with a full interpretation of the dream that had been shared with me. Did I care if I looked bad to the people listening to the show because I couldn't interpret every dream that was presented to me during the time? No I did not – from my perspective, as should be the case for all forms of evangelism, I am not an interpreter of dreams so that I look good. I interpret dreams to hopefully bring people closer to their Heavenly Father.

These have been a slection of some of the dreams and experiences that I have had the priveledge of interpreting over the last 15 years. I hope that you have found the information contained in this short book enlightening and that you will continue to seek out God in your dream life and grow in your ability to interpret the messages in the night.

All that is left is for me to do now is to bless you:
May you have sweet dreams from your loving Heavenly Father and understand the messages He is sending you as you sleep. May this bring a deeper intimacy to your relationship with Him.

OTHER RESOURCES:

If this book has whetted your appetite for learning more about the Biblical Method of dream interpretation then here are some resources that might help you:

www.streamsministries.com
Here you will find information about courses that you can take online or access 'live' around the world. I would highly recommend the 'Art of Hearing God ' and 'Understanding Dreams and Visions' courses, that's where I started.

www.thedreamhouse.co
This is my website where you will be able to send any dreams you would like interprete and also find links to other resources, such as articles and book recommendations.

ABOUT THE AUTHOR

Heather lives in Fife, Scotland with her family.

Heather is available to speak at events about dreams. If this is something that would interest you, or a group that you are part of, please contact her via The Dream House website.
heather@thedreamhouse.co

An Introduction to Biblical Dream Interpretation

Made in the USA
Monee, IL
07 December 2022